PATH TO PROSPERITY

PATH TO PROSPERITY

MARMADUKE ALVARADO

CONTENTS

CHAPTER 1

Introduction

Achieving financial security in today's world demands the acquisition of certain essential skills. These skills are not hidden away but are readily available to anyone ready to embrace the commitment required to master them. Unfortunately, many individuals choose to stay within their comfort zones, underestimating the effort needed to attain financial freedom. This introduction aims to break down these barriers and motivate you to embark on your journey toward financial independence.

You might wonder why so many people fail to achieve financial freedom despite its accessibility. The truth is, most people don't fully commit to the hard work required. They prefer the familiarity of their current situation over the uncertainty and effort involved in changing their financial circumstances. However, by reading this guide, you are already taking the first step towards change. As you progress through this book, your passion for financial independence will grow, and you will begin to experience the freedom you have been yearning for.

Consider the analogy of the Grand Canyon. Each year, around thirty million people from all corners of the globe visit this magnificent landmark. Yet, only about 250,000 manage to traverse the canyon fully, and some even require the assistance of park rangers to make it back. This scenario mirrors the journey to financial freedom. Many dream of it, but only a few persevere through the challenges to reach their goals. Human nature tends to favor comfort and observation over the hard work needed for significant change.

This guide is designed to help you overcome these tendencies and put you on a clear path to financial independence. Achieving financial freedom is a dream shared by many but realized by few. This book provides a step-by-step action plan to help you attain this goal. Be prepared for a challenging yet rewarding journey. Many people are willing to put in the work, invest wisely, and manage their investments effectively, but they often fall short because they fail to develop the necessary skills for financial security.

By the end of this guide, you will have a comprehensive understanding of the steps required to achieve financial independence. You will breathe the air of freedom that comes with financial security and feel the satisfaction of knowing that you have taken control of your financial future. Let's embark on this journey together, and transform your dreams into reality.

CHAPTER 2

Setting Financial Goals

In crafting your path to prosperity, setting clear and realistic financial goals is crucial. Each individual's journey is unique, influenced by their personal circumstances, career paths, and aspirations. Consider the contrasting examples of an oil-rig worker and a telecommunications equipment distributor in Portland, Oregon.

For the telecom distributor, a one-year goal could be to invest in telecom sales until it generates income that surpasses their current earnings. Meanwhile, an oil-rig worker might focus on building a sustainable, travel-based career over the next decade. This worker's immediate goal should be to showcase their skills and dedication to potential employers, highlighting their value in the telecom industry, even if their current savings strategy doesn't align perfectly with typical telecom investments.

As you organize your financial assets, keeping your goals at the forefront of your planning is essential. Follow these steps to craft a plan that leverages your strengths and opportunities:

1. **Assess Your Financial Net Worth**: Calculate your current financial status by summarizing all your assets and liabilities.

2. **Define Your Goals**: Ask yourself, "How much do I want to be worth?" Your goals need to be specific and realistic. Consider what your end result looks like in terms of:
     - **Retirement Expenses**: Aim for zero debt and a comfortable retirement.
     - **Lifestyle Aspirations**: Perhaps you dream of owning a vacation house in the Caribbean.
     - **Personal Acquisitions**: Maybe an extensive collection of antique mahogany furniture is what you envision.
     - **Philanthropy**: You might aim to establish a foundation that benefits a cause close to your heart.

The clearer your goals are, the better you can plan your path to achieving them.

Four Key Numbers to Consider in Your Financial Goals:

1. **Income**: What is your current income, and what do you aim for it to be?
2. **Expenses**: What are your current expenses, and how can you reduce them to increase savings?
3. **Savings**: What is your current savings amount, and what is your savings target?
4. **Investments**: What investments do you currently have, and what new investments can help you reach your financial goals?

Once you have these four key numbers in mind, you can start creating a step-by-step plan to reach your financial goals. Remember, your goals need to be both specific and realistic to be achievable.

By following these steps, you will be well on your way to financial independence. Setting financial goals is not just about dreaming but about creating a concrete plan that transforms those dreams into reality. Your journey to financial freedom begins with the clear vision of where you want to be and the unwavering commitment to get there.

CHAPTER 3

Creating a Budget

Strategically creating a budget is the foundation for growing your wealth and making your money work for you. A well-structured budget helps you manage your finances effectively, ensuring you meet your obligations and save for the future. Let's break it down step by step.

Start with Monthly Bills: The first step is to pay your monthly bills. Create a comprehensive list of all your bills, including rent or mortgage, utilities, insurance, groceries, and any other recurring expenses. When your paycheck comes in, compare the amounts to your paycheck and keep a schedule of when payments are due. Your goal should be to fully pay your monthly bills with one paycheck each month, regardless of how many paychecks you receive in a month. This approach ensures that one of your paychecks is dedicated solely to covering your essential expenses.

Savings Strategy: Once your monthly bills are covered by one paycheck, you can start saving the other one. Begin by educating yourself about various savings and investment options for retirement. Research 401(k) plans, small business retirement accounts, savings accounts, certificates of deposit (CDs), and other investment vehicles. Choose a combination of options that best fits your wealth goals and risk tolerance.

Budget Structure: After educating yourself, structure your budget to contribute to a savings or investment account each month. Some people may be able to save 20% of their income, but starting with 10% is common until you become more organized. Set up automatic transfers to move the money into your savings or investment account each month and then forget about it—let the money grow over time. Once you understand how much and when money is leaving your account, you can focus on saving the remaining 80%, minus any charitable donations.

Insurance Guidance: Michael Jordan, a licensed insurance agent for NJ, PA, DE, and MD, is a knowledgeable guide who can help you navigate your insurance options. She can educate you on selecting the best market for your business, securing a bond, deciding if a 401(k) is right for you, and choosing the right benefit package for your employees. As a minority woman-owned insurance agency, she understands the specific insurance needs of minority business owners. Whether your business is for-profit or non-profit, big or small, in the manufacturing industry, professional services, trade industry, retail, or food industry, she is here to serve you.

Creating a budget is not just about tracking expenses—it's about taking control of your financial future. By following these steps, you will be able to manage your finances more effectively, grow your wealth, and achieve your financial goals. The journey to financial independence starts with a solid budget plan, so take the time to create one that works for you.

CHAPTER 4

Saving and Investing

One crucial rule to achieving financial freedom is to invest your money wisely. The reality is, one day you may no longer wish to work, or circumstances might prevent you from working. It's essential to prepare for that time by making your money work for you.

Many people procrastinate, thinking they have plenty of time to start investing, or they shy away from it because they feel overwhelmed by the complexity of investments. This mindset is both harmful and misleading. Often, the real issue is a desire for the perceived security of an employee-to-employer relationship, which is ultimately not guaranteed. People claim that an employee's life is simple and without risk, but no job is safe from company downsizing, economic downturns, or market changes. Every day, thousands of jobs are lost, highlighting the importance of financial independence through investment.

The 30% Rule

Another vital principle to achieving financial freedom is the **30% rule**, which suggests saving 30% of your income. At first glance, this might seem like a daunting task, but consider this: if you don't save your money, what will you do with it? The rule encourages you to plan ahead, creating a financial cushion that can cover six months of expenses in case of emergencies.

Initially, saving 30% might seem challenging, and you may not be able to reach this target immediately. However, the goal is to gradually increase your savings until you can consistently set aside this amount. This method of intentional saving—planning with a purpose—makes it easier to save money once you have clear financial goals and a vision for your future.

Investing with Purpose

Investing is not just about saving money but about growing it. By investing wisely, you can create a sustainable source of income that will support you in the future. Here are some key points to consider when starting your investment journey:

1. **Educate Yourself**: Take the time to learn about different investment options such as stocks, bonds, mutual funds, real estate, and retirement accounts like 401(k) plans. Understanding these options will help you make informed decisions.
2. **Start Small**: You don't need to invest a large sum of money initially. Start with what you can afford and gradually increase your investments as you become more comfortable and knowledgeable.
3. **Diversify**: Spread your investments across different asset classes to minimize risk. Diversification helps protect your portfolio from market volatility.
4. **Set Goals**: Define your investment goals clearly. Whether it's saving for retirement, buying a house, or funding your children's education, having specific goals will guide your investment strategy.
5. **Stay Consistent**: Make investing a regular part of your financial routine. Set up automatic transfers to your investment accounts to ensure you consistently contribute to your future wealth.

The Role of a Financial Advisor

Consider seeking advice from a financial advisor. Professionals like Michael Jordan, a licensed insurance agent for NJ, PA, DE, and MD, can help you navigate the complexities of investing and insurance. She can provide guidance on selecting the best investment options, securing necessary bonds, and choosing suitable benefit packages for your employees. As a minority woman-owned insurance agency, she understands the unique needs of minority business owners and can tailor her advice to your specific situation.

CHAPTER 5

Managing Debt

To achieve financial freedom, it's crucial to free yourself from the burden of debt. Excessive debt not only limits your financial opportunities but also adds unnecessary stress to your life. Here are some essential strategies for effectively managing and reducing debt.

Understanding the Impact of Debt: First and foremost, recognize that accumulating debt can be a significant obstacle to financial freedom. Excessive debt restricts your ability to invest and grow your wealth. It's important to understand the consequences of debt and commit to strategies that minimize its impact on your financial health.

Strategies to Avoid Debt:

1. **Avoid Unnecessary Purchases**: The most straightforward strategy to avoid debt is to not purchase items you cannot afford. This simple tactic can save you from a lot of debt-related troubles. Before making any purchase, ask yourself if it's a necessity or a desire, and if you have the means to pay for it without resorting to credit.

2. **Eliminate Credit Cards**: Credit cards are often referred to as "the debt makers" of financial history. They can be tempt-

ing tools that lead to overspending and accumulating high-interest debt. Consider getting rid of your credit cards or at least limiting their use to emergencies only. This will help you avoid falling into the trap of revolving credit.

The 30% Rule: Another crucial rule in managing debt and achieving financial freedom is the **30% rule**, which suggests that you should save 30% of your income. While this might seem like a substantial portion, it's essential to anticipate future needs and build a financial cushion. Aim to save enough to cover at least six months of expenses in case of emergencies.

Practical Tips for Managing Debt:

1. **Create a Budget**: Developing a budget is a fundamental step in managing debt. List all your monthly expenses, including debts, and compare them to your income. Allocate funds to pay off your debts systematically while ensuring you cover your essential expenses.
2. **Prioritize Debt Repayment**: Focus on paying off high-interest debts first, such as credit card balances. Once these are under control, you can address other debts. Consider using methods like the snowball or avalanche approach to systematically reduce your debt.
3. **Save Before Spending**: If you can't afford something now, it means you don't have the money for it at the moment. Instead of acquiring debt, save up for your purchase. This approach not only helps you avoid debt but also instills a habit of saving.
4. **Seek Professional Advice**: Sometimes, managing debt can be overwhelming. Consider seeking advice from financial ad-

visors who can provide personalized strategies for debt management and financial planning.

Changing Your Financial Mindset: Understand that acquiring debt recklessly is akin to committing financial sabotage. Be smart and responsible about your financial decisions. If you plan to make a significant purchase in the future, save for it rather than relying on credit. This mindset shift will help you maintain control over your finances and work towards financial freedom.

Managing debt is a critical step on your journey to financial independence. By avoiding unnecessary debt, prioritizing debt repayment, and adopting a disciplined approach to spending and saving, you can build a solid financial foundation that supports your long-term goals.

CHAPTER 6

Building Multiple Streams of Income

One of the fundamental principles of achieving financial independence is creating multiple streams of income. Diversifying your income sources not only enhances financial stability but also accelerates wealth accumulation. Let's explore how to strategically build these income streams.

Active Income: Active income is the earnings you receive in exchange for your time and effort, such as your salary from full-time employment, freelancing, or active roles in a business. Establishing a strong foundation of active income is essential, as it provides the initial capital necessary for investments and further wealth-building endeavors. Active income funds your investments, grants you the freedom to pursue your dreams, and equips you with the knowledge needed to transition to other, less active income streams.

The Importance of Multiple Streams: Wealthy and successful individuals rarely rely on a single stream of income. Diversifying your income sources is a wiser and more stable approach. It helps protect against potential income loss and provides a safety net during economic fluctuations or unexpected life events. Building multiple streams of income might seem overwhelming initially, but starting early makes this task more manageable and beneficial in the long run.

Types of Income Streams:

1. **Earned Income**: Money earned from working actively in a job or business. This is your primary source of income when starting out.
2. **Profit Income**: Earnings from buying and selling goods, like running an e-commerce store or participating in the stock market.
3. **Interest Income**: Money earned from lending your money to others, such as through savings accounts, bonds, or peer-to-peer lending platforms.
4. **Dividend Income**: Earnings from owning shares in companies that pay dividends to their shareholders.
5. **Rental Income**: Money earned from renting out property, whether residential or commercial.
6. **Capital Gains**: Profits from selling investments, such as stocks, real estate, or other assets, at a higher price than you paid for them.
7. **Royalty Income**: Earnings from licensing your creative works, such as books, music, patents, or trademarks, to others.

Steps to Build Multiple Streams of Income:

1. **Start with Active Income**: Secure a reliable source of active income through full-time employment, freelancing, or running a business. This forms the base for your financial stability.

2. **Invest Wisely**: Use a portion of your active income to invest in various asset classes. Diversify your investments to spread risk and increase potential returns.

3. **Leverage Skills and Hobbies**: Identify skills or hobbies that can be monetized. For example, consider offering consulting services, creating online courses, or selling handmade products.

4. **Explore Passive Income Opportunities**: Invest in rental properties, dividend-paying stocks, or peer-to-peer lending platforms to generate passive income. These income streams require less active involvement once set up.

5. **Reinvest Earnings**: Continuously reinvest earnings from your various income streams to grow your wealth further. Compound interest and reinvestment can significantly accelerate wealth accumulation.

6. **Stay Informed and Adapt**: Keep abreast of market trends and continuously seek new income opportunities. Adapt your strategies to changing economic conditions and personal circumstances.

Building multiple streams of income is not as daunting as it may seem. There are numerous ways to establish both parallel and overlapping income sources, each contributing to a more secure and prosperous financial future. By diversifying your income, you create a resilient financial foundation that can weather life's uncertainties and pave the way to financial freedom.

CHAPTER 7

Building an Emergency Fund

An emergency fund is a crucial financial safety net that acts as a cushion during unexpected events such as job loss, medical emergencies, or other financial crises. By maintaining and regularly contributing to an emergency fund, you can ensure that you are prepared for life's uncertainties and avoid falling into financial distress.

The Importance of an Emergency Fund: An emergency fund serves as a buffer, allowing you to land on your feet when faced with unforeseen financial challenges. Those who have an emergency fund and contribute to it regularly rarely, if ever, experience financial calamity. The necessity of having an emergency fund cannot be overstated, and those who heed this advice often find themselves better prepared for life's unexpected twists and turns.

Learning from Others' Experiences: Many people only realize the importance of an emergency fund after experiencing a financial crisis. By spreading the word about the benefits of an emergency fund, we can help others avoid similar situations. Some individuals, humbled by life events, wish they had listened to this advice sooner. Avoiding commiseration and taking proactive steps to build an emergency fund can prevent financial calamities from worsening due to a lack of preparedness.

The Reality of Financial Preparedness: Despite the frequent advice to maintain an emergency fund, many people still have no money saved or invested at the time of a financial crisis. This lack of preparation often extends to covering basic necessities, leading to more severe financial issues. Understanding the necessity of an emergency fund is the first step towards safeguarding your financial future.

What Is an Emergency Fund?: An emergency fund is simply the perfect solution to life's uncertainties. These uncertainties, whether planned or unplanned, can significantly impact an individual's or family's finances. The primary purpose of an emergency fund is to prevent a temporary situation from becoming a more permanent financial setback. It keeps life's many crises from draining your financial resources.

Why Many People Are Not Proactive: Unfortunately, many people are not proactive when it comes to building an emergency fund. It's like watching someone about to be bitten by a snake when a clear warning sign is present. Most who get bitten fail to heed the warning. Some may turn angry and seek to blame others, but ultimately, it is a matter of personal oversight. Being forewarned about potential financial calamities is half the battle.

Steps to Building an Emergency Fund:

1. **Assess Your Monthly Expenses**: Calculate your monthly expenses, including rent/mortgage, utilities, groceries, transportation, and other necessities.
2. **Set a Savings Goal**: Aim to save enough to cover at least three to six months' worth of living expenses. This amount will serve as your financial cushion during emergencies.

3. **Create a Separate Savings Account**: Open a separate savings account specifically for your emergency fund. This helps you keep the funds separate from your regular spending money and reduces the temptation to dip into the fund for non-emergencies.

4. **Contribute Regularly**: Set up automatic transfers from your primary account to your emergency fund. Even small, consistent contributions can add up over time.

5. **Prioritize Your Emergency Fund**: Before making discretionary purchases, prioritize building your emergency fund. Once you reach your savings goal, you can allocate funds to other financial priorities.

6. **Avoid Using the Fund for Non-Emergencies**: Only use your emergency fund for genuine emergencies, such as job loss, medical bills, or unexpected major expenses. Resist the urge to dip into it for non-essential purchases.

Building an emergency fund is a proactive step toward financial security. By being prepared, you can mitigate the impact of life's uncertainties and ensure that temporary setbacks do not turn into long-term financial problems. Remember, being forewarned is forearmed—take the necessary steps today to protect your financial future.

CHAPTER 8

Protecting Your Wealth

A comprehensive wealth accumulation and preservation plan entails some form of protection and insurance. It's essential to safeguard your assets and income against unforeseen events. Let's delve into the various types of insurance you should consider to protect your wealth effectively.

Homeowners, Renters, and Auto Insurance: These types of insurance are common sense, yet many people take them for granted. Validate the quality of your insurance firsthand. Considering that your important assets will be parked there, do not skimp on the quality of your home insurance. Insure not just the house but also the replacement value of all your furnishings. Unfortunately, this is often the only way to ensure that insurance agents pay up in case of a claim.

Life Insurance: When it comes to life insurance, a common approach is to get all three: life, health, and disability insurance. Life insurance ensures that your dependents (children, and/or spouse) are financially protected if something happens to you. There are two main types of life insurance:

1. **Term Life Insurance**: Provides coverage for a specified period. It is generally more affordable and ideal if you have dependents who rely on your income.
2. **Permanent Life Insurance**: Offers lifelong coverage and has an investment component. However, it may not always be the best investment option.

According to financial expert Suze Orman, "Insure against the catastrophic, not the inconvenience." Be cautious of financing (paying interest) on your life insurance or other hidden costs. Ask for a customized comparative analysis of the top five best policies for each type of insurance.

Disability Insurance: This type of insurance is crucial, as it protects your most important asset—your income. If disability insurance is not covered by your employer, it's essential to get some form of coverage. Disability insurance ensures that you can maintain your financial stability in the event that you are unable to work due to illness or injury. Federal government employees, for example, have a group Long Term Care (LTC) Insurance plan, which can be a valuable benefit.

Long Term Care Insurance: Long Term Care Insurance (LTC) is designed to cover the costs of long-term care services, such as nursing homes or in-home care. For federal government employees, the Thrift Savings Plan (TSP) offers a limited general-purpose loan when they move to an inactive status. The TSP is considered the least expensive and most flexible LTC insurance available.

Health Insurance: Health insurance is essential for covering medical expenses and ensuring access to healthcare services. It's important to have a policy that suits your needs and provides adequate coverage for routine and emergency medical care.

Insurance Tips:

- **Do Your Research**: Compare different insurance policies to find the best coverage at the most affordable price. Ask for a comparative analysis to help you make an informed decision.
- **Understand Your Coverage**: Ensure you fully understand what is covered under your policy and any exclusions or limitations.
- **Review Regularly**: Regularly review your insurance policies to make sure they still meet your needs. Life changes such as marriage, children, or career advancements may require adjustments to your coverage.

Protecting your wealth through insurance is a proactive step towards financial security. By ensuring you have the right coverage for your assets and income, you can mitigate the impact of life's uncertainties and safeguard your financial future.

CHAPTER 9

Building a Retirement Plan

As we consider our approach to retirement, it's essential to acknowledge that living longer means planning for a more extended retirement period. With life expectancy on the rise, retiring at 65 could require funding 20-30 years of living expenses. If you choose to retire earlier, perhaps to be closer to your children and grandchildren, you'll need to prepare for an even longer retirement.

The Importance of Early Planning: Starting your retirement planning and savings early is crucial. Just as with career planning and purchasing a home, the sooner you begin, the easier it will be to reach your retirement goals. Open dialogue and consistent updates to your retirement plan can reduce discomfort when adjustments are necessary. Include the next generation in these discussions, as career and financial choices will increasingly be passed down through families.

Envisioning Your Retirement: The first step in mapping out your retirement is to envision what you want it to look like. While societal expectations have traditionally painted retirement as a time for travel and leisure, today's professionals can shape a retirement that suits their desires. Consider what activities bring you happiness and what is meaningful to you. Knowing these details allows you to plan appropriately for your retirement, whether your goal is to travel, volunteer, spend time with family, or continue working in a part-time role.

Breaking Down Your Retirement Goals:

1. **Activities-Based Planning**:
   - **Travel**: If you dream of traveling, research destinations, and estimate the costs involved. Consider how frequently you plan to travel and the associated expenses.
   - **Volunteering**: If giving back to the community is important to you, explore volunteer opportunities and any related costs, such as transportation or materials.
   - **Family Time**: If spending time with family is your priority, consider the costs of activities, family gatherings, and potentially providing financial support to your loved ones.
   - **Part-Time Work**: If you plan to continue working in some capacity, identify the type of work you enjoy and the income it may generate.
2. **Cost-Based Planning**:
   - **Housing**: Determine your housing needs and associated costs, whether you plan to downsize, relocate, or maintain your current residence.
   - **Healthcare**: Account for healthcare expenses, including insurance premiums, out-of-pocket costs, and long-term care.
   - **Lifestyle**: Estimate daily living expenses, such as groceries, utilities, transportation, and entertainment.
   - **Savings and Investments**: Calculate how much you need to save and invest to cover your retirement ex-

penses. Consider factors like inflation, market fluctuations, and potential changes in your lifestyle.

Including the Next Generation: Incorporate your family in your retirement planning discussions. Their understanding and support can make the transition smoother. Additionally, educating the next generation about financial planning ensures they are prepared for their future.

Regular Reviews and Adjustments: Regularly review and update your retirement plan to reflect changes in your goals, financial situation, or life circumstances. This proactive approach helps you stay on track and make necessary adjustments as needed.

Building a retirement plan is about creating a vision for your future and taking the necessary steps to achieve it. By planning early, envisioning your ideal retirement, and including your family in the process, you can create a fulfilling and secure retirement that reflects your aspirations.

CHAPTER 10

Estate Planning

Estate planning is a crucial part of managing your wealth, as it ensures that your assets are distributed according to your wishes and helps minimize the estate tax burden when you pass away. By utilizing various estate planning tools and strategies, you can protect your loved ones and provide for their future. Let's delve into some essential aspects of estate planning.

Minimizing Estate Taxes: To reduce the tax burden on your estate, consider using tools such as revocable living trusts, annual gifting, and properly titling assets. Many states impose their own estate taxes, so it's important to minimize both federal and state taxes. Every estate is unique, so it's advisable to speak with an estate planning attorney who can guide you according to the laws in your state.

The Importance of a Will: If you have assets to leave behind, it's imperative to have a will that clearly states who receives what upon your death. The complexity of your will may depend on the number of loved ones and the extent of your assets. At the very least, ensure you set "POD" (Payable on Death) designations on all your bank accounts. This designation acts as a beneficiary for your bank accounts, allowing your heirs to access funds for funeral expenses, bills, and other immediate costs without dealing with probate.

Life Insurance: Consider getting term life insurance, especially if you have dependents who rely on your income. Term life insurance provides financial support for your family for several years in the event of your unexpected death. This ensures that your loved ones are financially protected and can maintain their lifestyle.

Disability Insurance: Disability insurance is essential to protect your income, your most valuable asset. If your employer doesn't provide disability insurance, it's important to secure your own coverage. Disability insurance ensures that you can maintain financial stability if you become unable to work due to illness or injury.

Trusts for Minor Children: Setting up a trust for minor children is another important aspect of estate planning. Trusts allow you to manage and protect assets for your children until they reach adulthood. You can specify how and when the assets are distributed, ensuring that your children's needs are met.

Annual Gifting: Annual gifting is a strategy to reduce your taxable estate by giving gifts to your loved ones each year. The IRS allows you to gift a certain amount annually without incurring gift taxes. This not only reduces your estate tax burden but also allows you to see your loved ones benefit from your generosity during your lifetime.

Properly Titling Assets: Ensure that your assets are titled correctly. Proper titling can avoid probate and ensure a smooth transfer of assets to your heirs. For example, joint ownership with the right of survivorship allows property to pass directly to the surviving owner without going through probate.

Common Misconceptions: Some people put off estate planning because they don't like thinking about their death. However, taking the time to meet with an attorney and set things up properly can provide peace of mind. Knowing that your affairs are in order and that your loved ones will be taken care of can be quite comforting.

Steps to Effective Estate Planning:

1. **Consult an Attorney**: Work with an estate planning attorney to ensure your plan is legally sound and aligns with state laws.
2. **Draft a Will**: Clearly outline the distribution of your assets and designate guardians for minor children if applicable.
3. **Set Up Trusts**: Establish trusts to manage and protect assets for minor children or other beneficiaries.
4. **Designate Beneficiaries**: Assign "POD" designations on bank accounts and other financial assets.
5. **Consider Life and Disability Insurance**: Protect your income and provide for your dependents with appropriate insurance policies.
6. **Plan for Estate Taxes**: Utilize strategies like annual gifting and properly titling assets to minimize tax burdens.

Estate planning is a vital process that ensures your wealth is managed and distributed according to your wishes. By taking proactive steps and working with professionals, you can protect your loved ones and secure their financial future.

CHAPTER 11

Tax Planning Strategies

Tax planning is an essential component of increasing and preserving your wealth. Effective tax planning allows you to minimize your tax liability, ensuring that you retain more of your hard-earned money. Let's explore some key strategies and considerations for effective tax planning.

Understanding Tax Brackets: For context, here are the 2016 tax brackets for different filing statuses:

- **Single**:
    - $0 to $9,275 – 10%
    - $9,276 to $37,650 – 15%
    - $37,651 to $91,150 – 25%
    - $91,151 to $190,150 – 28%
    - $190,151 to $370,300 – 33%
    - $370,301 and above – 39.6%
- **Married Filing Jointly or Qualifying Widow(er)**:
    - $0 to $18,550 – 10%
    - $18,551 to $75,300 – 15%
    - $75,301 to $151,900 – 25%
    - $151,901 to $231,450 – 28%
    - $231,451 to $413,350 – 33%

- $413,351 and above – 39.6%
- **Married Filing Separately**:
  - $0 to $9,275 – 10%
  - $9,276 to $37,650 – 15%
  - $37,651 to $75,950 – 25%
  - $75,951 to $115,725 – 28%
  - $115,726 to $206,675 – 33%
  - $206,676 and above – 39.6%
- **Head of Household**:
  - $0 to $13,250 – 10%
  - $13,251 to $50,400 – 15%
  - $50,401 to $130,150 – 25%
  - $130,151 to $210,800 – 28%
  - $210,801 to $413,350 – 33%
  - $413,351 and above – 39.6%

While these figures are from 2016 and tax brackets may have changed, the concept of understanding where your income falls within these brackets remains crucial for effective tax planning.

The Importance of Tax Planning: Tax planning is one of the most critical steps in wealth management. The IRS requires information about your income and allows you to deduct certain expenses to lower your taxes. Although it may seem that some people pay more taxes than others, everyone pays taxes according to the legal options available. On a broader scale, the taxes paid often end up being quite fair for all. Billionaire Warren Buffett famously noted that he paid less in personal taxes than many of his employees, relatives, and friends, relative to the gains he achieved over his lifetime.

Key Tax Planning Strategies:

1. **Maximize Deductions and Credits**:

- **Itemize Deductions**: If your itemized deductions are greater than the standard deduction, itemize to reduce your taxable income.
- **Tax Credits**: Take advantage of tax credits, which directly reduce your tax liability. Examples include the Earned Income Tax Credit (EITC) and the Child Tax Credit.

2. **Contribute to Retirement Accounts**:
    - **401(k) and IRAs**: Contributions to retirement accounts like 401(k)s and IRAs are often tax-deductible. These accounts also grow tax-deferred until you withdraw the funds in retirement.
    - **Roth IRAs**: While contributions are not tax-deductible, Roth IRAs offer tax-free growth and tax-free withdrawals in retirement.

3. **Utilize Health Savings Accounts (HSAs)**:
    - Contributions to HSAs are tax-deductible, and withdrawals for qualified medical expenses are tax-free. HSAs also offer tax-deferred growth.

4. **Timing Income and Expenses**:
    - **Deferring Income**: If possible, defer income to a future year when you expect to be in a lower tax bracket.
    - **Accelerating Deductions**: Accelerate deductible expenses, such as charitable contributions or medical expenses, into the current year to maximize deductions.

5. **Invest in Tax-Advantaged Accounts**:
    - **529 Plans**: Contributions to 529 college savings plans may be state tax-deductible, and withdrawals for qualified education expenses are tax-free.

- ◦ **Municipal Bonds**: Interest income from municipal bonds is often exempt from federal income tax and may be exempt from state taxes as well.
6. **Seek Professional Advice**:
   - ◦ Tax laws can be complex and subject to change. Working with a tax professional can help you navigate these complexities and optimize your tax planning strategy.

Common Misconceptions: It's a common belief that some people pay more taxes than others, and that this is unfair. However, the tax system is designed to be as equitable as possible within the legal options available. By understanding and utilizing these options, you can ensure that you are paying your fair share while minimizing your tax liability.

Tax planning is a vital part of wealth management. By maximizing deductions, contributing to tax-advantaged accounts, and seeking professional advice, you can effectively manage your tax liability and enhance your financial well-being.

CHAPTER 12

Building a Strong Credit Score

Building a strong credit score is crucial for financial health and can significantly impact your financial opportunities. A higher credit score translates to lower interest rates, making loans and credit cards more affordable. Here's how you can build and maintain a strong credit score.

Understanding Credit Scores: Your credit score is a numerical representation of your creditworthiness, influencing your ability to obtain mortgages, car loans, and other forms of credit. The difference between a strong and a weak credit score can amount to hundreds of thousands, or even millions, of dollars in interest over the life of a loan.

Steps to Building a Strong Credit Score:

1. **Know Your Credit Score**:
    - Obtain your credit report from Equifax, Experian, and TransUnion. You can get these reports for free once a year at AnnualCreditReport.com
    - Familiarize yourself with the factors that determine your credit score and estimate your current range.

2. **Payment History (35%)**:
   - Payment history is the most significant factor in your credit score. Always pay your bills on time. If your score is currently poor or fair, consistently paying your bills on time for several years can significantly improve your score.

3. **Credit Utilization (30%)**:
   - This is the ratio of your current credit card balances to your credit limits. Aim to keep your credit utilization below 30%. If possible, pay off your credit card balances in full each month.

4. **Length of Credit History (15%)**:
   - The length of your credit history also affects your score. Keep older accounts open to maintain a long credit history.

5. **New Credit (10%)**:
   - Avoid opening multiple new credit accounts in a short period. Applying for new credit should be done sparingly and strategically. If possible, apply for new credit only once every two years.

6. **Credit Mix (10%)**:
   - A diverse mix of credit accounts (credit cards, mortgages, car loans) can positively impact your score. However, only take on new credit if necessary and manageable.

Practical Tips for Improving Your Credit Score:

- **Monitor Your Credit**: Regularly check your credit report for errors or inaccuracies and dispute any incorrect information.

- **Pay Down Debt**: Reduce your overall debt, focusing on paying off high-interest accounts first.
- **Limit Hard Inquiries**: Avoid unnecessary hard inquiries on your credit report, as they can temporarily lower your score.
- **Set Up Reminders**: Use payment reminders or automatic payments to ensure you never miss a due date.
- **Financial Responsibility**: Demonstrate responsible credit behavior over time to build and maintain a strong credit score.

Financial Freedom and Credit: A strong credit score is a key component of achieving financial freedom. It enables you to access better interest rates, which can save you substantial amounts of money over the life of loans and credit accounts. For example, over a 30-year term of a two million dollar loan, the difference between a strong and a weak credit score can mean paying up to $2,000,000 more in interest.

Retirement and Financial Goals: Financial freedom can take many forms, depending on individual life goals. For instance, early retirement is possible with good planning and potential sacrifices. According to studies, you need five million dollars to live comfortably in today's dollars if you retire between the ages of 35 and 65, expecting to live until 95. This assumes an 8% return on your five million dollars over your lifetime. The Financial Freedom Blueprint provides comprehensive strategies for achieving early retirement, covering eleven key areas: Control Debt and Spending, Make Money, Manage Investments, Preserve Health, Manage Taxes, Protect Assets (Estate Planning), Invest in Education, Network, Specialize, Create Business/Real Estate, and Improve Others.

Building a strong credit score is an ongoing process that requires diligence and financial responsibility. By understanding the factors that influence your credit score and taking proactive steps to improve it, you can pave the way towards a more secure and prosperous financial future.

CHAPTER 13

Maximizing Your Career Potential

As the economy improves and unemployment drops, companies will be on the lookout for talented, quality individuals. To stand out in this competitive job market, it's essential to maximize your career potential. Here are some strategies to help you get noticed and secure the job you desire.

Establishing an Online Presence: Start by creating a professional website that showcases your accomplishments, skills, and past job duties. Include videos and a portfolio of your work. Link your website to your LinkedIn and Facebook profiles. This gives employers a dedicated space to learn about your professional achievements before they look at your social media profiles.

Be mindful of what you post on social media. Avoid sharing political or controversial opinions on your Facebook page, as these do not concern potential employers and can complicate workplace dynamics.

Choosing the Right Company: Select a company that aligns with your values and goals. Look for organizations that use cutting-edge technology, innovate regularly, engage with their communities, and have a strong financial foundation. Avoid companies with a history of reverse layoffs, financial instability, or those that underpay and overwork their employees. Prioritize safety and ensure that the company provides a safe working environment.

Finding a Job You Love: If you already have a job you love, congratulations! If not, it's time to start looking for one that aligns with your passions, even if it means taking a lower-paying job initially. The fulfillment and satisfaction of doing work you enjoy will outweigh the temporary financial sacrifice.

Seeking Professional Guidance: If you're struggling to find a good job, consider meeting with a career counselor. They can provide valuable insights, tools, and mind-mapping software to help you identify suitable career paths and job opportunities. Recent college graduates should take online assessment tests (many of which are free) to identify career options that match their skills and interests. Once you know your strengths and the jobs that suit you, focus your job search on relevant companies within a reasonable distance from your home.

Leveraging Networking Opportunities: Networking is a powerful tool in job searching. Attend industry events, join professional organizations, and connect with people in your field. Networking can open doors to job opportunities that are not advertised publicly and can help you gain insights into potential employers.

Continuing Education and Skill Development: Invest in your professional development by continuing your education and acquiring new skills. This could involve taking online courses, earning certifications, or attending workshops. Staying up-to-date with industry trends and technologies will make you more attractive to potential employers.

Crafting a Strong Resume and Cover Letter: Your resume and cover letter are often the first impression you make on potential employers. Ensure that they are well-crafted, error-free, and tailored to the job you are applying for. Highlight your relevant skills, experience, and accomplishments.

Preparing for Interviews: Practice your interview skills by conducting mock interviews with friends, family, or a career counselor. Prepare answers to common interview questions and be ready to discuss your experience, skills, and why you are a good fit for the position.

Maximizing your career potential involves a combination of establishing a strong online presence, choosing the right company, finding a job you love, seeking professional guidance, leveraging networking opportunities, continuing education, crafting a strong resume and cover letter, and preparing for interviews. By taking these steps, you can enhance your career prospects and achieve your professional goals.

CHAPTER 14

Developing Financial Discipline

Financial discipline is a cornerstone of wealth-building. It involves making prudent financial decisions consistently, saving regularly, and avoiding unnecessary expenditures. Let's explore effective strategies for developing strong financial discipline.

Rewarding Financial Success: Larry Winget, in his book "You're Broke Because You Want To Be," suggests that people reward themselves after reaching specific savings milestones. For example, after saving $500, treat yourself to something you love. This positive reinforcement encourages continued savings and financial discipline. Winget also advises allocating half of any windfalls (unexpected income) to savings while allowing yourself to spend the other half on whatever you desire. This balanced approach ensures that you enjoy your financial gains while also building your savings.

The 20% Wealth Building Cycle: Developing financial discipline is part of the broader Wealth Building Cycle. By habitually saving a portion of your income and cutting off half of all windfalls for savings, you set the foundation for more advanced stages of wealth accumulation. Consistent saving and prudent financial management make it easier to achieve long-term financial goals.

The Power of Positive Reinforcement: Stephen Covey, a renowned author and speaker, emphasizes the importance of rewarding efforts to develop good habits. Even when individuals fall short of expectations, recognizing their efforts can motivate them to keep striving. Setting realistic goals based on individual or organizational capabilities and encouraging people to beat their personal best, rather than competing with others, fosters a supportive environment for growth.

The Finnish School System Model: The school system in Finland adopts a 'personal best' strategy, which emphasizes individual progress over competition. This approach results in various degrees of success rather than poor scores in examination results. By comparing personal performance to one's previous best, individuals are motivated to improve continuously without the pressure of competing against others.

Covey's Discipline Demonstration: In his estate planning seminar, Stephen Covey demonstrated the concept of discipline through a simple exercise. He asked participants to walk a straight line with their eyes open, which they all did successfully. When challenged to repeat the task with their eyes closed, many deviated. Covey then added an incentive: a $100 note at the end of the line. With the promise of a reward, most participants managed to walk straight without much deviation. This exercise illustrates that people are often disciplined by the hope of reward. By setting tangible rewards for financial milestones, you can enhance your financial discipline.

Practical Steps to Develop Financial Discipline:

1. **Set Clear Financial Goals**: Define your short-term and long-term financial objectives. Having clear goals provides direction and motivation.

2. **Create a Budget**: Track your income and expenses meticulously. A budget helps you understand where your money is going and identify areas where you can cut costs.

3. **Automate Savings**: Set up automatic transfers to your savings and investment accounts. This ensures that a portion of your income is saved before you have the chance to spend it.

4. **Avoid Impulse Purchases**: Practice mindful spending by avoiding impulse buys. Wait at least 24 hours before making non-essential purchases to determine if they are truly necessary.

5. **Monitor Progress**: Regularly review your financial progress. Celebrate milestones and adjust your strategies as needed to stay on track.

6. **Educate Yourself**: Continuously improve your financial knowledge. Read books, attend seminars, and seek advice from financial experts to make informed decisions.

Developing financial discipline requires consistent effort and a strategic approach. By rewarding your successes, setting realistic goals, and practicing mindful spending, you can build a strong foundation for financial stability and long-term wealth.

CHAPTER 15

Building a Support Network

Building a robust support network is vital for anyone on the path to financial independence. Surrounding yourself with like-minded individuals who share your goals can provide motivation, accountability, and valuable insights. Let's explore some strategies for creating and nurturing a supportive community.

The Lambo Retreat Model: One innovative approach to building a support network is the "Lambo Retreat" model. Every six months, members of the FL26 community from different parts of the country gather and rent a large vacation property. By sharing a beautiful, spacious, and occasionally quirky vacation home, participants save money, energy, and mental power while strengthening their partnerships. This cost-effective model allows for maximum lifestyle enhancement through shared experiences and collaborations.

Creating a Must-Spend-Time-With List: The financial independence community is known for its ability to enhance progress through collaboration. The FL26 2016 must-spend-time-with list was created to identify individuals who significantly contribute to your journey. Spending direct time with these people is invaluable.

Their support, knowledge, and encouragement can accelerate your path to financial independence.

The Lambo50 Retreat: In the fall of 2013, bloggers Ryan and Amanda Lange, Steve and Courtney Adcock, and Allison and I attended a retreat organized by our friends Jim and Lisa. We called it the Lambo50 retreat. The experience was so impactful that Jim and I later created our own podcast and decided to host a three-day meet-up. These gatherings allowed us to hatch future world domination plots while helping other financial independence seekers. Such retreats foster deep connections and provide a platform for sharing strategies and ideas.

The Power of Intimate Connections: At the March 2015 Camp FI, I had an enlightening conversation with Brian and Lynn from the blog "The Next Ten Words." Lynn emphasized that people working towards financial independence need intimate connection time with those pursuing similar goals. This insight resonated with me, and I took it to heart upon returning home. By prioritizing intimate connections, I experienced my most productive year of self-employment and happiness.

Practical Steps to Build a Support Network:

1. **Join Relevant Communities**:
    ◦ Participate in online forums, social media groups, and local meet-ups focused on financial independence. These platforms offer opportunities to connect with like-minded individuals.
2. **Attend Workshops and Conferences**:
    ◦ Attend events like Camp FI, FinCon, and other financial independence conferences. These gatherings provide valuable networking opportunities and a chance to learn from experts in the field.

3. **Create Your Own Meet-Ups**:
   - Organize local meet-ups or retreats with fellow financial independence seekers. These smaller, more intimate gatherings can foster deeper connections and more meaningful exchanges.
4. **Leverage Technology**:
   - Use tools like Zoom, Slack, and WhatsApp to stay connected with your support network, especially if members are geographically dispersed. Virtual meetings can maintain and strengthen relationships.
5. **Be Selective and Intentional**:
   - Surround yourself with individuals who inspire and challenge you. Be intentional about the people you spend time with and ensure they contribute positively to your journey.
6. **Engage in Mastermind Groups**:
   - Join or create mastermind groups where members regularly meet to discuss goals, share progress, and provide feedback. These groups offer accountability and diverse perspectives.

Conclusion: Building a strong support network is essential for achieving financial independence. By creating intentional connections, participating in meaningful gatherings, and leveraging the power of community, you can enhance your progress and enjoy a more fulfilling journey. Remember, the right support system can make all the difference in reaching your financial goals.

DIVERSIFYING YOUR INVESTMENTS

Diversification is a cornerstone of successful investing. It helps you build a robust asset base while minimizing risk. By spreading your investments across various assets and sectors, you reduce the impact of a poor performance in any single investment. Let's delve into effective strategies for diversifying your investments.

Start with Your Employer's Retirement Savings Plan: When you begin your career, you might be living paycheck to paycheck, with limited funds to invest. However, many employers offer retirement savings plans with company matching contributions. Participating in these plans is a great way to start building your investment portfolio. The earlier you start, the better, as you'll benefit from the power of compounding over time.

If you have access to a workplace retirement savings plan, sign up as soon as you're eligible and contribute as much as you can afford. Employer contributions can significantly boost your savings, so take full advantage of this benefit.

Why Diversification Matters: Diversification is crucial because it reduces the overall risk and volatility of your portfolio. Instead of putting all your money into one investment, you spread it across multiple investment types and companies. This way, if one investment performs poorly, your other investments can help balance out the losses.

Strategies for Diversification:

1. **Spread Across Asset Classes**:
   - **Stocks**: Invest in a mix of large-cap, mid-cap, and small-cap stocks across various industries.
   - **Bonds**: Include government, municipal, and corporate bonds to add stability and income to your portfolio.
   - **Real Estate**: Consider real estate investments, such as REITs (Real Estate Investment Trusts), to gain exposure to the property market.
   - **Commodities**: Invest in commodities like gold, silver, and oil to hedge against inflation and market volatility.
2. **Diversify Within Asset Classes**:
   - **Equities**: Invest in different sectors such as technology, healthcare, finance, and consumer goods.
   - **Bonds**: Include a mix of short-term, medium-term, and long-term bonds with varying credit ratings.
   - **Real Estate**: Diversify by investing in residential, commercial, and industrial properties.
3. **Geographic Diversification**:
   - **Domestic and International Investments**: Invest in both domestic and international markets to reduce geopolitical risks.
   - **Emerging Markets**: Consider investing a portion of your portfolio in emerging markets for higher growth potential.
4. **Investment Vehicles**:
   - **Mutual Funds and ETFs**: These funds allow you to invest in a diversified portfolio of stocks, bonds, or other assets with a single purchase.
   - **Index Funds**: Index funds track a specific market index, offering broad market exposure and lower fees.
5. **Alternative Investments**:

- ◦ **Private Equity**: Invest in private companies or start-ups for potential high returns.
- ◦ **Hedge Funds**: These funds use various strategies to generate returns, often uncorrelated with traditional markets.
- ◦ **Cryptocurrencies**: For those with a higher risk tolerance, consider allocating a small portion of your portfolio to cryptocurrencies.

Rebalancing Your Portfolio: Regularly review and rebalance your portfolio to maintain your desired asset allocation. As certain investments perform better than others, your portfolio can become unbalanced. Rebalancing ensures that you continue to adhere to your investment strategy and risk tolerance.

Conclusion: Diversifying your investments is essential for minimizing risk and achieving long-term financial goals. By spreading your investments across various asset classes, sectors, and geographic regions, you can build a resilient portfolio that can weather market fluctuations. Start with your employer's retirement savings plan and gradually implement these diversification strategies to grow your wealth securely.

CHAPTER 17

Real Estate Investing

Real estate can be a reliable and stable way to grow your wealth, especially if you plan to stay in one place for an extended period. However, for those who love to travel and prefer a more flexible lifestyle, investing in Real Estate Investment Trusts (REITs) can offer the benefits of real estate investments without the need to manage physical properties.

Real Estate Investment Trusts (REITs): REITs are investment funds that own and operate income-producing real estate. They distribute dividends to investors, similar to other investment products, but focus specifically on real estate. Investing in a portfolio of REITs that covers different market sectors—such as suburban residential units, industrial properties, and commercial real estate—allows you to maintain mobility while benefiting from the stability of real estate investments.

Advantages of REITs:

- **Diversification**: REITs allow you to invest in various types of real estate across different markets, reducing risk.
- **Liquidity**: Unlike physical properties, REITs can be bought and sold on the stock market, providing liquidity.

- **Income**: REITs typically pay regular dividends, providing a steady income stream.
- **Professional Management**: REITs are managed by professionals, eliminating the need for you to manage properties and tenants.

Direct Real Estate Investments: While REITs offer many benefits, direct real estate investments can also be a valuable addition to your portfolio. However, owning physical properties involves more hands-on management and potential risks.

Benefits of Direct Real Estate Investments:

- **Appreciation**: Real estate tends to appreciate over time, providing capital gains.
- **Control**: Owning property gives you control over its management and potential improvements.
- **Tax Benefits**: Real estate investors can take advantage of tax deductions for mortgage interest, property taxes, and depreciation.

Challenges of Direct Real Estate Investments:

- **Management Responsibilities**: Owning property involves managing tenants, maintenance, and repairs, which can be time-consuming and costly.
- **Market Volatility**: While real estate is generally more stable than stocks, property values can still fluctuate based on market conditions.
- **Liquidity Issues**: Selling property can take time, and you may not be able to access your investment quickly.

Comparing Real Estate to Stocks: While both real estate and stocks offer opportunities for appreciation and income, they differ in terms of volatility and management requirements. Stocks can be highly volatile, with prices fluctuating based on market conditions, company performance, and investor sentiment. Real estate, on the other hand, is often more stable and predictable, making it a safer investment for long-term wealth accumulation.

However, real estate investments come with their own set of risks, especially when managing physical properties. Tenants and property maintenance can turn assets into liabilities if not managed properly. Balancing the potential rewards with the responsibilities and risks is essential for successful real estate investing.

Conclusion: Real estate investing can be a powerful tool for wealth building, whether through direct property ownership or investing in REITs. By understanding the advantages and challenges of each approach, you can make informed decisions that align with your financial goals and lifestyle preferences. Diversifying your investments across different asset classes, including real estate, can provide stability and growth potential in your portfolio.

CHAPTER 18

Stock Market Investing

The stock market is often hailed as one of the best wealth-building tools, thanks to the power of compounding returns. Let's explore how stock market investing can help you build long-term wealth and how to get started.

The Power of Compounding: Compounding rates of return refer to the percentage by which a stock's price increases annually. For instance, the compound annual growth rate (CAGR) for the S&P 500 is about 9.8% over the long term. This means that if you invest in the S&P 500 and hold your investment for the next 20 years, you can expect an average annual return of 9.8% after factoring in inflation and taxes. The earlier you start investing, the more you can benefit from the compounding effect, as your returns will generate further returns over time. This principle is a key reason why the rich get richer, as larger sums of money have more potential to grow significantly over time.

Why Invest in the Stock Market: The stock market is an investor's paradise, offering a great way to build long-term wealth with relatively low risk. History has shown that, over the long term, stocks are the best-performing asset class. However, many people hesitate to invest in stocks due to perceived risks and a lack of knowledge about how to get started. It's important to remember that, while stocks are not risk-free, they offer higher potential returns compared to savings accounts, which often grow at a rate lower than inflation.

Key Principles for Stock Market Investing:

1. **Start Early**:
    ◦ The earlier you start investing, the more time your money has to grow. Even small investments can compound significantly over decades.

2. **Diversify Your Portfolio**:
    ◦ Diversification is crucial to managing risk. Spread your investments across various sectors and asset classes to reduce the impact of poor performance in any single investment.

3. **Invest for the Long Term**:
    ◦ Stock market investing is best suited for long-term goals. Avoid trying to time the market, and instead, focus on holding quality investments over the long term.

4. **Reinvest Dividends**:
    ◦ Reinvesting dividends can significantly enhance your returns over time. Many companies offer dividend reinvestment plans (DRIPs) that allow you to automatically reinvest your dividends.

5. **Educate Yourself**:
    ◦ Take the time to learn about the stock market, different types of stocks, and investment strategies. This knowledge will help you make informed decisions and build confidence in your investments.

Getting Started with Stock Market Investing:

1. **Open an Investment Account**:

- To buy stocks, you need to open a brokerage account. Many online brokers offer user-friendly platforms with educational resources to help you get started.

2. **Set Investment Goals**:
   - Define your investment goals, whether it's saving for retirement, buying a home, or building an emergency fund. Your goals will guide your investment strategy.

3. **Choose Your Investments**:
   - Start with broad-based index funds or ETFs (exchange-traded funds) that track the performance of major market indices like the S&P 500. These funds offer diversification and are relatively low-cost.

4. **Automate Your Investments**:
   - Set up automatic contributions to your investment account to ensure consistent investing. Dollar-cost averaging, where you invest a fixed amount regularly, can help mitigate market volatility.

5. **Monitor and Rebalance Your Portfolio**:
   - Regularly review your portfolio to ensure it aligns with your goals and risk tolerance. Rebalance your portfolio periodically to maintain your desired asset allocation.

Conclusion: Stock market investing is a powerful tool for building long-term wealth. By starting early, diversifying your investments, and focusing on long-term goals, you can harness the power of compounding returns to achieve financial success. Educate yourself, stay disciplined, and take advantage of the opportunities the stock market offers.

CHAPTER 19

Building a Business

The principle of building a business as a pathway to financial freedom is straightforward. Business has always been, and will always be, a powerful platform for wealth creation. Let's explore the different types of business structures and their potential for earning.

The Power of Entrepreneurship: When I first decided to break free from financial constraints, I turned to the internet for guidance. Initially, I encountered a mix of people trying to sell me something. However, as I delved deeper, I discovered the real key to financial freedom: starting a business. It's a lot of work, but business offers unparalleled opportunities for financial independence.

Types of Business Structures:

1. **Sole Proprietorship**:
    - **Overview**: A sole proprietorship is the simplest form of business structure, where one person owns and operates the business. This type of business is easy to set up and gives the owner complete control.
    - **Earning Potential**: While sole proprietorships can be highly profitable, they also carry personal liability for debts and obligations. Success often depends on the

owner's ability to manage and grow the business effectively.

2. **Partnership**:
     - **Overview**: A partnership involves two or more individuals who share ownership and operation of the business. Partnerships can combine the skills and resources of multiple people, leading to potentially greater earning potential.
     - **Earning Potential**: Profits are shared among partners according to the partnership agreement. While partnerships can be lucrative, it's crucial to have clear agreements to avoid conflicts and ensure smooth operations.

3. **Corporation**:
     - **Overview**: A corporation is a more complex business structure that is legally separate from its owners. It offers limited liability protection and can raise capital through the sale of stock.
     - **Earning Potential**: Corporations have significant earning potential, especially if they grow and attract investors. However, they also face more regulatory requirements and administrative responsibilities.

Starting a Side Business: You don't need to start a megacorporation to achieve financial freedom. Starting a side business can be a great way to supplement your income and build wealth. This approach allows you to maintain your current job while exploring entrepreneurial opportunities.

Steps to Starting a Business:

1. **Identify Your Business Idea**:

- Consider your skills, interests, and market demand. Choose a business idea that aligns with your passions and has potential for growth.

2. **Conduct Market Research**:
   - Research your target market, competitors, and industry trends. Understanding the market landscape will help you develop a solid business plan.

3. **Create a Business Plan**:
   - A business plan outlines your business goals, strategies, and financial projections. It serves as a roadmap for your business and can help you secure funding.

4. **Register Your Business**:
   - Choose a business name and register it with the appropriate government authorities. Depending on your business structure, you may also need to obtain licenses and permits.

5. **Secure Funding**:
   - Determine your startup costs and explore funding options, such as personal savings, loans, or investors. Having adequate capital is crucial for launching and growing your business.

6. **Set Up Your Operations**:
   - Establish your business operations, including location, equipment, and technology. Ensure you have systems in place for managing finances, marketing, and customer service.

7. **Launch and Promote Your Business**:
   - Once everything is set up, launch your business and promote it to your target audience. Use marketing strategies like social media, advertising, and networking to attract customers.

Conclusion: Building a business is a powerful way to achieve financial freedom. Whether you choose to start a sole proprietorship, partnership, or corporation, entrepreneurship offers countless opportunities for growth and wealth creation. By starting a side business, you can gradually transition to full-time entrepreneurship and enjoy the benefits of financial independence.

CHAPTER 20

Creating Passive Income Streams

Creating passive income streams is essential for achieving financial freedom. Passive income refers to money that works for you, allowing you to generate income with minimal active effort. By diversifying your sources of passive income, you can build a stable and reliable financial foundation. Let's explore various passive income sources and how to leverage them effectively.

Understanding Passive Income: Passive income is derived from activities in which you do not materially participate. This includes rental income from properties, dividends from stock investments, interest from savings accounts, and other income sources that do not require ongoing work. The key to passive income is that your money continues to generate income for you, allowing you to pursue your goals and enjoy financial freedom.

Key Passive Income Sources:

1. **Dividend Growth Investing**:
   - Dividend growth investing involves buying stocks that regularly pay dividends and have a history of increasing their payouts. This strategy allows you to build a port-

folio that generates a steady stream of income. Many investors work with a Certified Public Accountant (CPA) to design withdrawal methods that maximize income with minimal effort once retirement begins. U.S. tax-advantaged investment accounts can also help stretch your retirement resources.

2. **Real Estate Investments**:
   - **Rental Properties**: Owning rental properties provides a reliable source of passive income. Rental income can cover property expenses and generate additional cash flow.
   - **Real Estate Investment Trusts (REITs)**: REITs allow you to invest in real estate without owning physical properties. They distribute dividends to investors, providing a steady income stream.
   - **Home Equity**: Home equity can be a valuable asset that generates rental income or can be leveraged for further investments.

3. **Interest from Savings Accounts and Money Market Accounts**:
   - Although interest rates on savings accounts and money market accounts are relatively low, they still provide a safe and stable source of passive income. These accounts are essential for preserving capital while earning interest.

4. **Pension Savings**:
   - Pensions provide a guaranteed income stream in retirement. Contributing to pension plans throughout your career can ensure a reliable source of income in your later years.

5. **Tax-Advantaged Investment Accounts**:

- Investing in tax-advantaged accounts such as IRAs and 401(k)s allows your money to grow tax-free or tax-deferred. These accounts can provide significant income in retirement.

Building a Diversified Passive Income Portfolio: To achieve financial freedom, it's important to diversify your passive income sources. This reduces risk and ensures a steady income stream regardless of market conditions. Here are some steps to build a diversified passive income portfolio:

1. **Identify Your Income Goals**:
   - Determine how much passive income you need to achieve financial freedom. This will guide your investment strategy and asset allocation.
2. **Create a Balanced Portfolio**:
   - Diversify your investments across different asset classes, such as stocks, bonds, real estate, and alternative investments. This balance helps mitigate risk and maximize returns.
3. **Automate Your Investments**:
   - Set up automatic contributions to your investment accounts. Automation ensures consistency and takes advantage of dollar-cost averaging.
4. **Reinvest Your Earnings**:
   - Reinvest dividends, interest, and rental income to compound your returns. This accelerates the growth of your passive income over time.
5. **Monitor and Adjust Your Portfolio**:

- Regularly review your portfolio to ensure it aligns with your income goals and risk tolerance. Make adjustments as needed to optimize performance.

Conclusion: Creating passive income streams is a powerful strategy for achieving financial freedom. By investing in dividend growth stocks, real estate, savings accounts, pensions, and tax-advantaged accounts, you can build a diversified portfolio that generates steady income with minimal effort. The key is to start early, automate your investments, and continually reinvest your earnings. With a solid passive income strategy, you can enjoy financial security and pursue your dreams with confidence.

CHAPTER 21

Investing in Mutual Funds

Investing in mutual funds is a powerful strategy for achieving your long-term financial goals. Mutual funds allow you to diversify your investments across a wide range of assets, which can help reduce risk and increase potential returns. Let's dive into the essentials of mutual fund investing and how to integrate it into your financial plan.

Understanding Mutual Funds: A mutual fund is a pool of money collected from multiple investors to invest in a diversified portfolio of stocks, bonds, or other securities. Each investor owns shares of the mutual fund, representing a portion of the fund's holdings. Professional fund managers oversee the fund's investments, making decisions based on the fund's objectives and strategies.

Benefits of Investing in Mutual Funds:

1. **Diversification**:
    - Mutual funds offer instant diversification by investing in a wide range of securities. This reduces the risk of significant losses from any single investment.
2. **Professional Management**:

- ◦ Experienced fund managers handle the investment decisions, saving you the time and effort required to research and manage individual investments.

3. **Accessibility**:
   - ◦ Mutual funds are accessible to individual investors, often with lower minimum investment requirements compared to other investment vehicles.

4. **Liquidity**:
   - ◦ Mutual funds can be bought and sold on any business day, providing liquidity and flexibility for investors.

Creating an Investment Policy Statement (IPS): To guide your mutual fund investments, create an Investment Policy Statement (IPS). This document outlines your investment goals, risk tolerance, time horizon, and asset allocation strategy. An IPS serves as a roadmap for your investment decisions, helping you stay focused on your long-term objectives.

Evaluating Key Investment Choices: As part of your comprehensive investment strategy, evaluate the following investment choices that typically dominate an investor's portfolio:

1. **Employer 401(k) Plans**:
   - ◦ Take advantage of employer-sponsored retirement plans, which often include matching contributions. Maximize your contributions to benefit from tax-deferred growth.

2. **Individual Retirement Accounts (IRAs)**:
   - ◦ IRAs offer tax advantages for retirement savings. Consider both Traditional and Roth IRAs based on your current tax situation and future expectations.

3. **Defined-Benefit Pension Plans**:

- If you have access to a pension plan, understand its benefits and how it fits into your overall retirement strategy.

4. **Self-Employment Retirement Plans**:
   - For self-employed individuals, explore Solo 401(k) or SEP IRA plans to maximize retirement savings.

5. **Health Savings Accounts (HSAs)**:
   - HSAs provide triple tax advantages: tax-deductible contributions, tax-free growth, and tax-free withdrawals for qualified medical expenses.

6. **529 College Savings Plans**:
   - These plans offer tax advantages for saving for education expenses. Contributions grow tax-free, and withdrawals for qualified expenses are also tax-free.

Measuring Investing Success: The true measure of your investing success is not merely the change in your bank and investment account balances but your progress toward your long-term financial goals. Achieving financial freedom, as you define it, is the ultimate goal. A positive change in your investment account value is encouraging, but the focus should remain on reaching the income goals necessary for your current and future spending needs.

Conclusion: Investing in mutual funds is a versatile and effective way to build a diversified portfolio and achieve your long-term financial goals. By creating an Investment Policy Statement, evaluating key investment choices, and focusing on your financial objectives, you can navigate the world of mutual fund investing with confidence. Remember, the measure of your success is your progress toward financial freedom, not just the fluctuations in your account balances.

CHAPTER 22

Planning for Education Expenses

The cost of post-secondary education continues to rise, making the prospect of funding your children's college education a daunting task. However, with careful preparation and wise financial decisions, you can mitigate these expenses and make higher education more affordable. Let's explore strategies for effective education expense planning.

Seek Out Low-Cost Education Options: One way to reduce out-of-pocket school expenses is to explore low-cost education options coordinated with your in-state university. In-state tuition rates are often significantly lower than out-of-state rates, providing substantial savings. Additionally, community colleges can offer a cost-effective start to higher education, allowing students to complete general education requirements before transferring to a four-year institution.

Understand Financial Aid: College financial aid works inversely to what many people expect. The more assets you appear to have, the less financial aid you may receive. Proper care must be taken in how you save for college to maximize the amount of aid your student may receive. Here are some key points to consider:

1. **Free Up Available Money**:
    - Families, except for the wealthiest, should prioritize freeing up available money first. This approach gives students a better chance at receiving financial aid by reducing the appearance of available assets.
2. **Financial Aid Formulas**:
    - Understand how financial aid formulas work. The Expected Family Contribution (EFC) is calculated based on your income, assets, and other factors. Lowering your EFC can increase your eligibility for need-based aid.
3. **Strategic Timing of Withdrawals**:
    - Plan the timing of withdrawals from college savings accounts carefully. Drawing from these accounts too close to when you need the funds can negatively impact financial aid eligibility.

Types of College Savings Plans: Consider various college savings plans that offer tax advantages and flexibility:

1. **529 College Savings Plans**:
    - 529 plans allow you to invest in a tax-advantaged account for future education expenses. Earnings grow tax-free, and withdrawals for qualified expenses are also tax-free.
2. **Coverdell Education Savings Accounts (ESAs)**:
    - ESAs provide tax-free growth for education expenses. Unlike 529 plans, ESAs have lower contribution limits but offer more flexibility in investment choices.
3. **Custodial Accounts (UGMA/UTMA)**:

∘ These accounts allow you to save and invest money for your child's education. However, assets in these accounts are considered the student's assets, which can impact financial aid eligibility.

Scholarships and Grants: Encourage your child to apply for scholarships and grants. These funds do not need to be repaid and can significantly offset education costs. Research local, state, and national scholarship opportunities, and consider both merit-based and need-based options.

Health Care Costs and Retirement: When planning for education expenses, it's also essential to consider the broader financial picture, including potential health care costs in retirement. Health care expenses are a growing concern for retirees, and unexpected medical costs not covered by insurance can threaten financial security. Additionally, affordable and accessible housing that allows retirees to age in place must be factored into the financial plan. Home modifications and services like food delivery or lawn maintenance are often unanticipated expenses that can add to monthly housing costs.

Start Saving Early: The earlier you start saving for your child's education, the better. Starting early allows you to take advantage of compound interest and build a substantial education fund over time. Encourage your child to participate in saving for their education by setting aside a portion of their earnings from part-time jobs or allowances.

Conclusion: Planning for education expenses requires a strategic approach and early action. By exploring low-cost education options, understanding financial aid, utilizing college savings plans, and starting early, you can make higher education more affordable and secure your child's future. Remember to also consider the impact of health care and housing costs on your long-term financial security.

CHAPTER 23

Minimizing Expenses

Minimizing expenses is an essential aspect of achieving financial freedom. By reducing unnecessary costs and adopting mindful spending habits, you can free up more resources to save and invest. Let's explore effective strategies for minimizing expenses and maximizing financial efficiency.

Contemplating Space Before Purchases: Before making any new purchases, consider the implications of space. Fewer tables, bookcases, chairs, and other nonessential household items translate into lower cleaning, replacement, repair, and maintenance costs. This approach helps ease household stress and reduces overall expenses.

Visualizing and Reviewing Savings Goals: Regularly visualize and review your reasons for saving, especially during a 12-month fast. This practice helps you stay focused on your goals, even when faced with challenges or contrasting objectives. In critical moments, will you stay steadfast in integrating creativity and action, or will you succumb to nonessential activities for comfort? Sometimes, compromise is necessary. Respect nonessential items by celebrating holidays or birthdays meaningfully, without materialistic decorations. Celebrate with simple, heartfelt gestures, such as preparing freshly baked cookies, which can create a unique connection with the receiver.

Keeping a Budget: Maintaining a budget is a cornerstone of minimizing expenses. Set a clear financial goal, such as saving for a down payment on a new home within the next twelve to eighteen months. Make this goal an unwavering commitment. To do this, take inventory of your household expenses using a financial blueprint sheet. Write down monthly and one-time expenses, and identify areas where you can cut costs.

Three-Month Budget Fast: Challenge yourself to a three-month budget fast by living with less for an extended period. Highlight, circle, or mark expenses on your financial blueprint sheet that you can live without for three months or more. These expenses may include utilities, cable, internet, groceries, eating out, entertainment, clothing, transportation, insurance coverage, and education club memberships. This exercise helps you identify nonessential expenses and adopt more frugal habits.

Eliminating Nonessential Space: Consider the issue of space and eliminate nonessential areas. Unused water heaters, closet space, spare rooms, furniture, and garden space result in higher living costs. Living upfront with less takes practice, but it can significantly reduce expenses. Remember the 80/20 principle: most higher expenses stem from 20 percent of your household items. Focus on reducing the most burdensome 20 percent of your expenses.

Accumulating Essentials: Gather household items from what you already own or buy used or discounted quality items to fill your home with essentials. This approach helps you avoid unnecessary purchases and maintain a minimalist lifestyle.

Practical Steps to Minimize Expenses:

1. **Review Subscriptions and Memberships**:

- Cancel any subscriptions or memberships that you no longer use or can live without. This includes streaming services, gym memberships, and magazine subscriptions.

2. **Cook at Home**:
   - Prepare meals at home instead of dining out. Cooking at home is often more cost-effective and healthier.

3. **Use Public Transportation**:
   - If possible, use public transportation, carpool, or bike instead of driving. This can save money on fuel, maintenance, and parking.

4. **Shop Smart**:
   - Use coupons, buy in bulk, and shop during sales to reduce grocery and household expenses.

5. **Reduce Energy Usage**:
   - Implement energy-saving practices, such as using LED bulbs, unplugging devices when not in use, and setting your thermostat to energy-efficient temperatures.

6. **DIY Repairs and Maintenance**:
   - Learn basic DIY skills to handle small repairs and maintenance tasks around the house, reducing the need for professional services.

Conclusion: Minimizing expenses is about making mindful choices and adopting frugal habits. By contemplating space before purchases, visualizing savings goals, maintaining a budget, and eliminating nonessential space, you can significantly reduce your living costs. These strategies not only free up resources for saving and investing but also contribute to a more organized and stress-free lifestyle.

CHAPTER 24

Understanding Insurance Policies

Insurance policies are a critical component of any comprehensive financial plan. They provide protection against unforeseen events and financial risks, ensuring that you and your loved ones are safeguarded. Let's explore the various types of insurance that matter most and why they are essential.

David's Essential Insurance Types:

1. **Life Insurance:**
   - **Term Life Insurance:** Term life insurance is cost-effective and provides coverage for a specified period. It's ideal for individuals who have dependents or significant financial obligations. It's recommended to purchase a policy that aligns with the term of your financial plan. Most people need term life insurance when they have young children or other dependents.

2. **Health Insurance:**
   - Health insurance covers medical expenses, including doctor visits, hospital stays, and prescription medications. Having adequate health insurance is crucial to

protect against high medical costs and ensure access to necessary healthcare services.

3. **Long-Term Disability Insurance**:
   - This insurance provides income replacement if you become unable to work due to a long-term disability. It's essential to protect your most valuable asset—your ability to earn an income.

4. **Homeowner's and Renter's Insurance**:
   - **Homeowner's Insurance**: Covers damage to your home and personal property, as well as liability for accidents that occur on your property.
   - **Renter's Insurance**: Provides coverage for personal property and liability for renters. It's affordable and protects against losses due to theft, fire, and other disasters.

5. **Auto Insurance**:
   - Auto insurance is mandatory in most states and covers damage to your vehicle, liability for bodily injury or property damage, and medical expenses resulting from accidents.

6. **Personal Liability Insurance**:
   - Personal liability insurance protects you from financial loss if you are found legally responsible for causing injury to someone or damaging their property.

7. **Umbrella Liability Insurance**:
   - This insurance provides additional liability coverage beyond the limits of your homeowner's, auto, and other liability policies. It's an extra layer of protection against large claims and lawsuits.

8. **Long-Term Care Insurance**:

○ Long-term care insurance covers the cost of long-term care services, such as nursing home care, in-home care, and assisted living. It's essential for protecting your savings and ensuring access to quality care in your later years.

The Importance of Proper Insurance: As highlighted by financial expert David Bach, having the right insurance is crucial. Even if you have a well-structured investment system, lacking adequate insurance can leave you vulnerable to financial disaster. Proper insurance provides a safety net that protects your assets, income, and overall financial well-being.

Key Considerations When Choosing Insurance:

1. **Assess Your Needs**:
    ○ Evaluate your financial situation, dependents, and potential risks to determine the types and amounts of coverage you need.

2. **Compare Policies**:
    ○ Shop around and compare policies from different insurers. Look for comprehensive coverage at competitive rates.

3. **Understand Policy Details**:
    ○ Carefully read the terms and conditions of each policy. Understand what is covered, exclusions, and any limitations.

4. **Seek Professional Advice**:
    ○ Consult with a financial advisor or insurance agent to ensure you choose the right policies for your needs and financial goals.

Conclusion: Understanding and securing the right insurance policies are vital steps in protecting your financial future. By covering various aspects of your life, from health and income to property and liability, you can safeguard yourself and your loved ones against unforeseen events. Prioritize insurance as a fundamental part of your financial plan to achieve peace of mind and long-term financial security.

CHAPTER 25

Creating a Will

Creating a will is a crucial yet often overlooked aspect of financial planning. Many people postpone drafting a will for various reasons, such as thinking they don't have enough assets or feeling too young to need one. However, having a will is essential for everyone, regardless of age or asset level. Let's explore why creating a will is important and how to go about it.

Common Misconceptions: In places like Singapore, many people believe they don't have enough assets to justify creating a will. However, most individuals own more than they realize. Consider assets like money in the Central Provident Fund (CPF), life insurance policies, and bank account balances. Additionally, thinking about one's mortality can be uncomfortable and often leads to procrastination. Some people also perceive wills to be costly, further delaying the process. In reality, creating a will is often very affordable, especially for expats who may have more complex situations.

The Importance of a Will: It's often said that the only certainties in life are death and taxes. While contemplating one's mortality can be unpleasant, it's an inevitable part of life. Without a will, you cannot control how your estate—everything you own—is distributed after your death. This can lead to complications and stress for your loved ones. A will ensures that your assets are distributed according to your wishes and provides peace of mind.

Steps to Creating a Will:

1. **Assess Your Assets:**
   - Take inventory of your assets, including bank accounts, investments, property, CPF savings, life insurance policies, and personal belongings. This will help you understand what you need to include in your will.

2. **Choose Your Beneficiaries:**
   - Decide who will inherit your assets. Beneficiaries can include family members, friends, or charitable organizations. Clearly specifying your beneficiaries prevents disputes and ensures your wishes are followed.

3. **Appoint an Executor:**
   - The executor is responsible for carrying out the instructions in your will. Choose someone you trust to manage your estate, pay any debts, and distribute assets to your beneficiaries.

4. **Consider Guardians for Minor Children:**
   - If you have minor children, appoint a guardian to care for them in your absence. This is a crucial decision that ensures your children's well-being.

5. **Consult a Solicitor:**
   - Working with a solicitor helps navigate the complexities of creating a will. A professional ensures that your will is legally sound and accurately reflects your wishes. Mistakes in a will can be costly for those left behind, making professional guidance invaluable.

6. **Keep Your Will Updated:**

○ Life circumstances change, so it's important to review and update your will regularly. Significant life events, such as marriage, divorce, the birth of children, or acquiring new assets, may necessitate changes to your will.

Cost Considerations: Contrary to popular belief, creating a will is often inexpensive. The cost varies depending on the complexity of your estate and the solicitor's fees, but it is generally a worthwhile investment. For expats and those with more complex financial situations, the benefits of having a properly drafted will far outweigh the costs.

Conclusion: Creating a will is a vital step in securing your financial future and ensuring your wishes are honored after your death. It provides peace of mind for you and your loved ones, knowing that your estate will be managed according to your instructions. Don't put off this important task—take the time to create a will and protect your legacy.

CHAPTER 26

Retirement Account Options

When planning for retirement, it's essential to understand the various retirement account options available to you. These accounts offer different tax advantages and can significantly impact your long-term financial security. Let's explore the most common retirement account options and their key features.

401(k) Plans:

- **Traditional 401(k)**: These accounts allow you to save a portion of your salary before taxes are deducted. The money is taken out of your paycheck pre-tax, and you don't owe taxes until you withdraw the funds in retirement. This can be advantageous if you're currently in a high tax bracket and expect to be in a lower tax bracket after retirement. Employers often contribute to traditional 401(k) plans, providing additional savings.

- **Roth 401(k)**: Unlike traditional 401(k) accounts, Roth 401(k) contributions are made with after-tax dollars. This means you pay taxes on the money now, but qualified withdrawals in retirement are tax-free. Roth 401(k) accounts are beneficial for younger employees who expect to be in a higher tax bracket later in life. Employers may also contribute to Roth 401(k) accounts, but their contributions are taxed upon withdrawal.

Individual Retirement Accounts (IRAs):

- **Traditional IRA**: Contributions to a traditional IRA are often tax-deductible, reducing your taxable income for the year. The money in the account grows tax-deferred, meaning you don't pay taxes on investment gains until you withdraw the funds in retirement. This can be a good option if you expect to be in a lower tax bracket in retirement.
- **Roth IRA**: Contributions to a Roth IRA are made with after-tax dollars, so they are not tax-deductible. However, the money grows tax-free, and qualified withdrawals in retirement are also tax-free. Roth IRAs are ideal for individuals who anticipate being in a higher tax bracket in retirement.

Self-Employment Retirement Plans:

- **Solo 401(k)**: Designed for self-employed individuals and small business owners with no employees, Solo 401(k) plans allow for higher contribution limits and tax advantages. You can contribute both as an employer and an employee, maximizing your retirement savings.
- **SEP IRA (Simplified Employee Pension)**: SEP IRAs are another option for self-employed individuals and small business owners. Contributions are tax-deductible, and the account grows tax-deferred until retirement.

Health Savings Accounts (HSAs):

- HSAs offer triple tax advantages: contributions are tax-deductible, the money grows tax-free, and withdrawals for qualified medical expenses are also tax-free. HSAs can be an effective way to save for future healthcare costs in retirement.

529 College Savings Plans:

- While not specifically for retirement, 529 plans offer tax advantages for saving for education expenses. Contributions grow tax-free, and withdrawals for qualified education expenses are also tax-free. This can help reduce the financial burden of funding your children's education.

457 Plans:

- 457 plans are deferred compensation plans available to government employees and some non-profit employees. Contributions are tax-deferred, and the money grows tax-free until withdrawn in retirement.

Key Considerations:

- **Tax Treatment**: Determine whether you want to save with traditional, tax-deferred dollars or after-tax dollars. Traditional accounts offer tax deductions on contributions, while Roth accounts provide tax-free growth and withdrawals.
- **Employer Contributions**: Take advantage of any employer matching contributions, as this is essentially free money added to your retirement savings.

- **Investment Choices**: Understand the investment options available within each account and choose those that align with your risk tolerance and retirement goals.

Conclusion: Understanding the different retirement account options and their tax implications is crucial for effective retirement planning. Whether you choose a traditional 401(k), Roth IRA, or other retirement accounts, the key is to start saving early and consistently. By leveraging these accounts and their tax advantages, you can build a robust retirement portfolio and achieve long-term financial security.

CHAPTER 27

Investing in Cryptocurrencies

Cryptocurrencies have taken the world by storm, sparking interest from all corners of society. Initially used by the black market, cryptocurrencies have gained mainstream attention and are now considered by many as a legitimate investment option. Let's delve into the fundamentals of investing in cryptocurrencies and the revolutionary technology behind them.

The Innovation of Blockchain Technology: Blockchain technology, introduced by Bitcoin, is often compared to the internet in terms of its revolutionary impact. The primary innovation of Bitcoin is not just the cryptocurrency itself, but the underlying Distributed Ledger Technology, commonly known as the blockchain. This technology allows data to be stored across a network of thousands of computers, enabling secure and transparent transactions.

Key Advantages of Blockchain:

1. **Transparency and Security**:
    - Blockchain ensures that everyone on the network knows who owns how much money at any given time. The decentralized nature of the blockchain makes it

nearly impossible to fake transactions, as every transaction is verified by multiple nodes on the network.

2. **Resilience**:
   - The decentralized network is virtually impossible to shut down. If a government blocks access to Bitcoin, users can continue their transactions from another location where Bitcoin is allowed, ensuring uninterrupted business operations.

3. **Trustless Transactions**:
   - Blockchain removes the need for intermediaries like banks by allowing direct peer-to-peer transactions. This trustless system relies on cryptographic algorithms and consensus mechanisms to verify and record transactions, reducing reliance on centralized institutions.

The Rise of Cryptocurrencies: Cryptocurrencies were introduced in 2009 by an individual or group under the pseudonym Satoshi Nakamoto, who launched Bitcoin. The primary purpose was to revolutionize the transaction process by bypassing banks, resulting in lower transaction fees, faster transactions, and decreased reliance on traditional financial institutions.

Notable Cryptocurrencies:

1. **Bitcoin (BTC)**:
   - Bitcoin is the first and most well-known cryptocurrency. It serves as a digital currency and a store of value, often referred to as "digital gold."

2. **Ethereum (ETH)**:
   - Ethereum is a decentralized platform that enables smart contracts and decentralized applications (dApps). Its

native currency, Ether, is used to power transactions and computational services on the network.

3. **Litecoin (LTC)**:
   ◦ Often considered the "silver to Bitcoin's gold," Litecoin offers faster transaction times and a different hashing algorithm.

4. **Ripple (XRP)**:
   ◦ Ripple focuses on enabling real-time cross-border payments for financial institutions, providing a faster and more cost-effective alternative to traditional banking systems.

Investment Considerations:

1. **Volatility**:
   ◦ Cryptocurrencies are known for their price volatility. While this can offer significant profit potential, it also comes with higher risk. Investors should be prepared for price fluctuations.

2. **Regulatory Environment**:
   ◦ The regulatory landscape for cryptocurrencies is still evolving. Investors should stay informed about legal and regulatory developments that may impact the market.

3. **Security**:
   ◦ Security is paramount in cryptocurrency investing. Investors should use secure wallets and exchanges, enable two-factor authentication, and be cautious of phishing attacks and scams.

4. **Diversification**:

- Diversifying your cryptocurrency portfolio can help mitigate risk. Consider investing in a mix of established cryptocurrencies and promising new projects.

5. **Long-Term Perspective**:
   - While short-term trading can be profitable, adopting a long-term perspective allows investors to ride out volatility and benefit from the overall growth of the cryptocurrency market.

Conclusion: Investing in cryptocurrencies offers the potential for significant returns, but it also comes with inherent risks. Understanding the revolutionary blockchain technology, the key advantages of cryptocurrencies, and the considerations for investing can help you make informed decisions. Stay informed, practice due diligence, and approach cryptocurrency investing with caution to build a resilient and diversified portfolio.

Managing Financial Risks

Managing financial risks is essential for ensuring the stability and growth of your investments. Authoritative and binding financial advice, particularly related to retirement income and investment strategies, should rely on the scientific method. This approach involves well-defined objectives, data analysis, and testable predictions to validate investment methods, such as the 4% rule. Let's delve into why managing financial risks matters and explore various types of risks and strategies to mitigate them.

Why Managing Financial Risks Matters: Effective risk management ensures that your savings and investments are available when you need them. Whether saving for your children's college expenses or preserving wealth for retirement, protecting your assets from market volatility is crucial. If you are retired and relying on your wealth, managing risks ensures that you won't run out of money.

Interest Rate Risks: Bonds lose value when interest rates increase. This risk can impact the value of your bond investments and overall portfolio. To manage interest rate risks, consider diversifying your investments across different maturities and types of bonds.

Real Estate Market Risk: The real estate market can be volatile. A market collapse can turn a seemingly solid real estate investment into a poor one. Diversifying your real estate investments and conducting thorough market research can help mitigate this risk.

Country Risk: Political instability, war, hyperinflation, or adverse government policies can drastically reduce the value of your investments in a particular country. To manage country risk, diversify your investments geographically and consider investments in stable economies.

Business Risk: Even stable businesses can become less profitable, go bankrupt, or disappear entirely, reducing their stock price to zero. To mitigate business risk, diversify your investment portfolio across different industries and companies.

Stock Market Risk: Stock prices can be unpredictable. A good company may see its stock price plummet due to market conditions or internal issues. Diversifying your investments and employing a long-term investment strategy can help manage stock market risk.

Types of Financial Risks: Here are four primary categories of financial risks:

1. **Market Risks**:
    - Market risks are associated with fluctuations in the financial markets. This includes stock market risk, interest rate risk, and real estate market risk.
2. **Credit Risks**:
    - Credit risks arise when borrowers fail to repay their loans. This can impact investments in bonds and other fixed-income securities.
3. **Liquidity Risks**:
    - Liquidity risks occur when you are unable to sell an investment quickly without significantly reducing its price. This can affect real estate and certain stocks.
4. **Operational Risks**:

- Operational risks are related to internal failures within a company, such as management errors, fraud, or system failures.

Strategies for Managing Financial Risks:

1. **Diversification**:
   - Diversify your investments across different asset classes, industries, and geographic regions. This reduces the impact of poor performance in any single investment.
2. **Asset Allocation**:
   - Allocate your investments based on your risk tolerance, investment goals, and time horizon. A balanced mix of stocks, bonds, and other assets can help manage risk.
3. **Regular Review and Rebalancing**:
   - Regularly review your investment portfolio and rebalance it to maintain your desired asset allocation. This ensures that your portfolio remains aligned with your financial goals.
4. **Risk Assessment**:
   - Continuously assess the risks associated with your investments. Stay informed about market conditions, economic trends, and company performance.
5. **Use of Hedging**:
   - Consider using hedging strategies, such as options and futures, to protect your investments from market volatility.

Conclusion: Managing financial risks is crucial for achieving long-term financial stability and growth. By understanding different types of risks and implementing effective risk management strategies, you can protect your investments and ensure that your financial goals are met. Remember, the key to successful risk management is diversification, regular review, and a proactive approach to identifying and mitigating potential risks.

CHAPTER 29

Building a Strong Financial Foundation

The starting point for our journey towards financial freedom is the development and commitment to your unique operational framework, known as the Operational Blueprint. This blueprint serves as your comprehensive plan for gaining financial control and addressing life's financial threats. The process of creating your Operational Blueprint should be both logical and emotional, requiring investment in time and effort. Completing these initial steps will provide you with the focus needed to overcome financial challenges—an essential prerequisite for building a successful life.

Creating Your Operational Blueprint: Your personal Operational Blueprint will identify clear, strategic, and tactical solutions to each financial threat, along with prioritized plans for achieving them. This blueprint will guide you in incorporating the tools, techniques, and strategies that balance your spending desires while maximizing the efficiency of your greatest asset: Your Money Making Machine. By successfully executing your Operational Blueprint, you can integrate modern financial tools and techniques, leading to significant and reliable results.

Laying the Groundwork: Just as you need to walk before you can run, you must establish a strong financial foundation before building a secure financial future. The first part of the Financial Freedom Blueprint focuses on laying this groundwork. Decades of experience have shown that without a solid foundation, individuals cannot fully benefit from the ideas, techniques, and technologies available to them on their journey to financial freedom. For example, handing a teenager the keys to a Formula One race car without any driving experience would be foolish. Instead, you would help them master the fundamentals of driving, ensuring they are well-prepared to compete at the highest levels.

Components of a Strong Financial Foundation:

1. **Budgeting and Saving**:
    - Creating a budget is the cornerstone of financial planning. Track your income and expenses, identify areas where you can cut costs, and prioritize saving. Building an emergency fund with at least three to six months' worth of living expenses is crucial.

2. **Debt Management**:
    - Addressing and reducing high-interest debt is essential for financial stability. Develop a plan to pay off credit card debt, student loans, and other liabilities. Consider using strategies like the snowball or avalanche method to accelerate debt repayment.

3. **Insurance and Risk Management**:
    - Protecting yourself and your assets with appropriate insurance is vital. Ensure you have health, life, disability, and property insurance to mitigate financial risks.

4. **Retirement Planning**:

- Start saving for retirement as early as possible. Contribute to employer-sponsored retirement plans, such as 401(k)s, and individual retirement accounts (IRAs). Take advantage of employer matching contributions and tax-advantaged accounts.

5. **Investment Strategy**:
   - Develop a diversified investment strategy that aligns with your risk tolerance and financial goals. Consider a mix of stocks, bonds, real estate, and other asset classes to spread risk and maximize returns.

6. **Estate Planning**:
   - Creating a will and establishing an estate plan ensures that your assets are distributed according to your wishes. Consider setting up trusts and assigning beneficiaries to protect your legacy.

Implementing Modern Tools and Techniques: Integrating modern financial tools, toys, and techniques can enhance the effectiveness of your Operational Blueprint. Utilize budgeting apps, investment platforms, and financial planning software to streamline your financial management processes. These tools can help you track progress, make informed decisions, and stay on top of your financial goals.

Conclusion: Building a strong financial foundation is essential for achieving long-term financial success. By developing your Operational Blueprint, mastering the fundamentals of financial management, and incorporating modern tools and techniques, you can create a secure and prosperous financial future. Remember, the key to financial freedom is a solid foundation, strategic planning, and disciplined execution.

CHAPTER 30

Tracking and Evaluating Your Progress

Tracking and evaluating your financial progress is crucial for achieving long-term financial goals and attaining financial freedom. By regularly assessing your financial status, you can identify areas for improvement and make informed decisions to accelerate your financial achievements. Let's explore the key steps to effectively track and evaluate your progress.

Calculating Turnover Percentage: The turnover percentage measures the profit or loss from your assets over time. To calculate this percentage:

1. Find the balance recorded for each kind of investment.
2. Calculate the interest percentage obtained concerning the balance.
3. Consider the previous balance recorded and the income earned within a specific period.
4. Evaluate the turnover percentage on a yearly or tri-monthly basis for consistent tracking.

Calculating Savings Balance: To evaluate your savings balance:

1. Point out the interest collected in all savings accounts.
2. Exclude paid interests on loans unless the activity is related to wealth generation through money lending-borrowing.
3. Record how much interest has been paid to you, allowing you to evaluate the turnover percentage allocated to lending-borrowing.
4. Include zakat funds and monitor any bad debts. There is no need to input reimbursed loans in the account.

Steps to Track and Evaluate Financial Progress:

1. **Set Clear Financial Goals:**
   - Define short-term and long-term financial goals. These goals provide a clear direction and help you stay focused on your financial journey.
2. **Create a Budget:**
   - Maintain a detailed budget to track your income and expenses. This helps you identify spending patterns, reduce unnecessary expenses, and allocate funds towards savings and investments.
3. **Monitor Investments:**
   - Regularly review your investment portfolio. Calculate the turnover percentage and assess the performance of each investment. Make adjustments as needed to align with your financial goals.
4. **Track Savings:**
   - Keep a close eye on your savings accounts. Monitor interest earned and ensure you are meeting your savings targets. Regularly update your records to reflect any changes.
5. **Evaluate Debt Management:**

○ Review your debt repayment progress. Ensure you are on track with paying off high-interest debts and consider strategies to accelerate debt repayment.

6. **Review Net Worth**:
   ○ Calculate your net worth periodically. This involves subtracting your liabilities from your assets. Tracking your net worth helps you understand your overall financial health and progress.

7. **Adjust Strategies**:
   ○ Based on your evaluations, adjust your financial strategies as needed. This may involve reallocating investments, increasing savings, or implementing new debt management techniques.

8. **Seek Professional Advice**:
   ○ Consider consulting with a financial advisor to gain expert insights and ensure you are on the right path. Professional guidance can help you optimize your financial strategies and achieve your goals more efficiently.

Conclusion: Tracking and evaluating your financial progress is essential for achieving financial freedom. By calculating turnover percentages, monitoring savings, and regularly reviewing your financial status, you can make informed decisions to enhance your financial well-being. Stay committed to your financial goals, make necessary adjustments, and seek professional advice to ensure long-term success.

CHAPTER 31

Overcoming Financial Obstacles

A money shortage when it comes to saving is often more about how you organize your finances than how much you make each month. Achieving a prosperous life filled with accomplishments requires mastering more than just saving. It's about becoming someone who constantly seeks self-improvement, strives for excellence in everything they do, values people, and commits to delivering their best every single day. Simply put, it's hard to see someone bankrupt while sitting on millions in the bank, highlighting that financial freedom is not just about having money but understanding its true value and purpose.

Understanding Savings: To save means to take a part of your income and guarantee it for future use. This concept ensures the longevity of your earnings. If you don't grasp this, you might think working more to earn more money is the solution to saving. However, if you are not saving from what you have now, you won't save from any additional money you receive later.

The Secret to Prosperity: If you aspire to become successful in your career and stand out in your chosen field, professionalism must be part of your journey. This involves always giving more than you receive. I firmly believe that this is the great secret of life: being willing to do whatever it takes to achieve excellence and being committed to continuous self-improvement.

The Savings Dilemma: Many people think they cannot save because they look for "spare" money to save instead of saving from their current income. They view their income as what is left to spend, including the money they save. This mindset guarantees saving difficulties. The key is to adopt the logic of paying yourself first: save first and spend thereafter. This small change—prioritizing saving as the top priority instead of a bottom priority—enables anyone to save money.

Steps to Overcoming Financial Obstacles:

1. **Budgeting**:
    ◦ Create a detailed budget that tracks your income and expenses. Identify areas where you can cut back and allocate a portion of your income to savings.

2. **Pay Yourself First**:
    ◦ Treat your savings as a non-negotiable expense. Set up automatic transfers to your savings account as soon as you receive your paycheck. This ensures that saving becomes a habit.

3. **Set Clear Financial Goals**:
    ◦ Define specific financial goals, such as building an emergency fund, saving for a down payment on a home, or planning for retirement. Clear goals provide motivation and direction.

4. **Reduce Debt**:
    ◦ Focus on paying off high-interest debt as quickly as possible. Reducing debt frees up more money for saving and investing.

5. **Increase Your Income**:
    ◦ Look for opportunities to increase your income, such as taking on a side job, freelancing, or seeking a promotion at work. Additional income can accelerate your savings goals.
6. **Stay Disciplined**:
    ◦ Avoid impulse purchases and unnecessary spending. Stick to your budget and savings plan, even when it's challenging.
7. **Seek Professional Advice**:
    ◦ Consider consulting with a financial advisor to develop a personalized financial plan. Professional guidance can help you navigate complex financial decisions and stay on track.

Conclusion: Overcoming financial obstacles requires a mindset shift and disciplined financial habits. By understanding the true meaning of saving, prioritizing your financial goals, and continuously striving for excellence, you can build a prosperous and financially secure future. Remember, the secret to financial freedom lies in consistently giving your best and making informed, intentional financial decisions.

Conclusion

In this personal finance guide and roadmap to wealth building, we have aimed to provide a dense, self-contained education on how the big-picture of money and wealth works. It is our firm belief that understanding the whole empowers each part with integrity, clarity, and directness. After digesting these Foundations of Finance, you can move on to the blueprints and strategies for wealth: the main body of the text. Let's delve into the logical fabric that stitches our understanding of money and wealth from the first principles. Our task in the foundation chapters has been to develop an understanding of our financial world from the most basic concepts, including the definitions of finance, money, and wealth.

Adopting this financial freedom blueprint is one of the best investments you can make. Mastery of these specific ideas will empower you to make informed and intelligent decisions in both practical and financial estate-planning areas. It is also our hope that through the lens of these thoughts, you will not only gain new insights into personal finance and investments, but also be encouraged to live a more purposeful and balanced life. How many people do you know who are so consumed and obsessed with money, work, and other "things of importance" that they neglect their own and their family's well-being?

By embracing the principles and strategies outlined in this guide, you can avoid falling into this trap. Instead, you can achieve financial freedom while maintaining a healthy and fulfilling life. Remember, the journey to financial freedom is not just about accumulating wealth, but also about finding balance and purpose in every aspect of your life.

As you move forward, keep these key takeaways in mind:

- **Financial Education**: Continuously educate yourself about personal finance and investments.
- **Goal Setting**: Set clear, achievable financial goals and create a plan to reach them.
- **Discipline and Consistency**: Stay disciplined in your financial habits and be consistent in your efforts.
- **Balance**: Strive for a balanced life that prioritizes both financial success and personal fulfillment.
- **Adaptability**: Be prepared to adapt your strategies as circumstances change, and always be open to learning and growth.

We hope this guide has provided you with the tools, knowledge, and inspiration needed to embark on your journey to financial freedom. May you find success, happiness, and balance in all your endeavors.